the electronic keyboard collection book 3

Selected and edited by Jeremy Ward

Faber Music 3 Queen Square London WC1N 3AU
in association with
Trinity Guildhall 89 Albert Embankment London SE1 7TP

Contents

© 2005 by Faber Music Ltd and Trinity College *London*

First published in 2005 by Faber Music Ltd

in association with Trinity College London

3 Queen Square London WC1N 3AU

Cover design by Sue Clarke

Music processed by Jackie Leigh

Printed in England by Caligraving Ltd

All rights reserved

ISBN 0-571-52354-4

To buy Faber Music or Trinity publications or to find out about the full range of titles
available please contact your local music retailer or Faber Music sales enquiries:

Faber Music Ltd, Burnt Mill, Elizabeth Way, Harlow CM20 2HX

Tel: +44 (0)1279 82 89 82   Fax: +44 (0)1279 82 89 83

sales@fabermusic.com   fabermusic.com   trinitycollege.co.uk

Theme from Symphony No.40

Wolfgang Amadeus Mozart (arr. Ward)

Voice: Strings/Orch Horns
Style: 8 Beat Modern

Mozart composed 41 symphonies and this is one of his most famous. The melody, played by the strings, must feel full of energy, with long, *legato* bowed phrases. Pay attention to the rests and don't forget the accents. When the horns are added, think about adding another accompaniment level as well.

Mamma Mia

**Stig Anderson／Benny Andersson／
Bjoern Ulvaeus (arr. Ward)**

This hit by Abba contains a lot of different ideas. The opening needs to be tightly controlled *staccatos*: be careful not to rush. The melody that follows it needs to have a sweeping feel, but the eighth notes (quavers) in bars 7–8 need to be played rhythmically like an accompaniment. Try using different voices and accompaniment levels to show the different musical ideas.

Voice: Piano/Fire Wire, Strings
Style: Rock

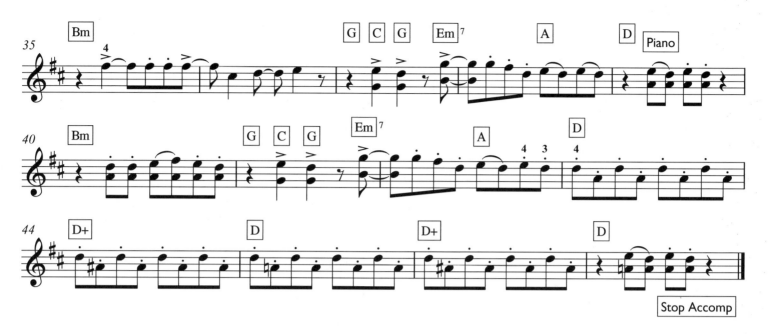

Greek Dance

Composition project

Voice: Own Choice
Style: Own Choice

You need to select a voice, style and dynamics and also develop some ideas to make this piece complete. Greek music is very rhythmic so make sure this has a sense of movement throughout. It also relies on repetition, so develop the existing ideas rather than creating new melodies. You could keep this very traditional or bring it up-to-date with your choice of voice: the melody will still sound Greek in style.

With bounce ♩ = 120-140

The Swan

Camille Saint-Saëns (arr. Ward)

Voice: Harp/Strings, Oboe/Strings
Style: Guitar Serenade or Waltz

The Swan was written as part of a larger work called 'The Carnival of the Animals' and portrays a swan gliding elegantly by. The *legato* phrasing is very important and the dynamic changes are achieved by the different voices. The *staccato* ending should sound like the first drops of a summer shower: nothing heavy, just a few spots!

Recharge!

Pam Wedgwood

Voice: Big Band Brass
Style: Big Band Swing

This is a 1950s big band piece and it opens with strong brass theme: don't rush it. It is the type of tune that big bands would play as their signature tune, the tune that the band was famous for. Take care of the articulation: the brass players would tongue the accented notes very clearly.

Detroit Soul

Jeremy Ward

> Voice: Pop Brass/Hyper Brass,
> Growl Sax/Sax Sect
> Style: Detroit Pop or Pop

This style goes back to the 1960s gospel music of Black America. It is very energetic and rhythmical and needs to be swung. The opening brass idea is based on a fanfare and needs to be strong and confident. The saxophone melody at bar 18 needs to imitate a singer and bar 28 is the chorus, so add the saxophone section. At bar 52 the piece moves up a tone to increase the excitement: the brass fanfare will sound brighter in this key.

Hogmanay Party

Traditional and Jeremy Ward

Voice: Tubular Bells, Bagpipes, Recorder, Fiddle
Style: Scottish Reel

As New Year approaches, bells ring out and a bagpiper strikes up *Auld Lang Syne*: make sure you don't rush this section. At the end of this tune a recorder player enters with a Scottish dance, and it doesn't take long before the partygoers are dancing and whirling round the floor. This piece needs an even and well-controlled right hand. There is little time to add more than is asked, but the speed and excitement will make it a concert favourite.

On the Savannah

Jeremy Ward

Voice: Flute/Dream Heaven, Strings,
Orch Horns, Oboe
Style: Movie Ballad or Ballad

The scene is the African savannah: a vast expanse of land with wild animals roaming there. The warm theme at the beginning soars and must be played *legato*, imitating the animals moving across the plain. The sunrise is shown by the move into A minor and by adding horns and another accompaniment level if you can. The scene now is of a vast array of animals and the scenery is bathed in brilliant sunlight.

Under Arrest

Jeremy Ward

Voice: Big Lead/Hyper Brass or Pop Brass
Style: 70s Pop or Funk

Imagine a police thriller TV series in the 1970s: lots of energy and quick scene changes of chases, car races, arrests and explosions. The opening is very tight and *staccato*, with a great chord sequence. The slurred sixteenth note (semiquaver) passage at bar 13 increases the tension and must be played rhythmically. The melody in the middle needs to be confident and bold: make sure you don't rush it.

Christmas Crackers Medley

Traditional (arr. Ward)

Voice: Pipe Organ, Trumpet/Brass Sect,
Glockenspiel/Strings, Trombone
Style: Modern 8 beat

This collection of Christmas favourites begins seriously with 'O Come All Ye Faithful'. Gradually thoughts turn to fun and snow with a jazzy version of 'Jingle Bells' and 'Good King Wenceslas'. A more serious introduction of 'While Shepherds Watched' is quickly interrupted with a chorus of 'We Wish You A Merry Christmas'. Just before the end the first tune comes back and the peel of Christmas bells can be heard. Try different voices and styles here to add different flavours to the pieces.

While Shepherds Watch

Don't Cry for Me Argentina

Music by Andrew Lloyd Webber (arr. Ward)
Lyrics by Tim Rice

Voice: Oboe/Strings, French Horns
Style: Musical Ballad or Ballad

This famous tune comes from the hit musical 'Evita'. In this song, Evita appears on the balcony to make a speech to the waiting crowd. The atmosphere is a little hesitant, as she is not sure how the crowd will react. Try to make it sound thoughtful, with *legato* phrasing. As the crowd warms to what she is saying the confidence grows, with the introduction of chords and the instruments. Finally there is a big *crescendo* to the chorus.